TICO SLANG

Learning Costa Rican Spanish OneWord at a Time

Edited by Timothy P. Banse

TICO SLANG
Learning Costa Rican Spanish One Word at a Time

ISBN-13: 978-0934523547 (Middle Coast Publishing)
ISBN-10: 0-934523-54-1

Editor@Middle-Coast-Publishing.com

Front Cover photo, Plaza de la Central, San Jose, Costa Rica, by Eric T. Gunther, licensed under, CC BY-SA 3.0
https://creativecommons.org/licenses/by-sa/3.0/

Back cover photo, Red-eyed Tree frog, photographed near Playa Jaco, Costa Rica, by Carey James Balboa, Public domain.

Middle-Coast-Publishing.com

Dedicated a la pura vida!

Aa

¡Al chile! – Really! Seriously!
¡Arriba las manos! - Hands up!
A culo pelado – Nude, naked.
A gas pegado – At full speed.
A la gringa - The American way.
A la hora de burro – To arrive very late.
A la par – Next to.
A la parilla – Grilled.
A la plancha – Sautéed.
A manos llenas – By the handful.
A mecate corto – On a short leash. to curtail freedom.
A medias – To share costs or to go fifty-fifty.
A medias, ni mis medias – To do something halfway.
A medio palo – To do something half–assed or half-way.
A pata – On foot.
A puro gúevo – By force, under duress.
A su gusto – To your liking.
A toda madre – Something good.
A toda máquina – At full speed.
A toda vela – At full speed.
A toda velocidad – At full speed.
A todo gas - To do something at full speed,
Abrir una cuenta – To run a tab.
Abrirse – To leave or to go.
Abue - 1. Abbrev for abuelo/abuela – grandparent. 2. Rocking chair.
Achantado – Disappointed. disenchanted.
Achantarse – To be lazy, lethargic, or to not feel like doing anything.
Achará – To be a pity.
Acois – Right here, this place.
Acribillar – To riddle with bullets.
Adiós – A greeting, often used to simply say, hello.
Aflojar – To pay.
Agachado – Unmotivated.
Agarrado – A stingy person, a cheapskate.
Agarrar cancha – To take advantage of, or to gain experience.

Agarrar con las manos en la masa – To catch red-handed.
Agarrar de chanco – To pull somone's leg or to fool or spoof.
Agarrar de mae - To be made a fool of.
Agarrar de mona – To pull someone's leg (figurative).
Agarrar el mensaje - To get the hint or to catch on.
Agarrar volados – To learn.
Agarrarla toda – To have good luck or success.
Agarrarse – To fight.
Agazapado – A hypocrite.
Agringado – To exhibit the customs and manners of a gringo.
Agringarse - To be Americanized in habits or customs.
Agua dulce – A drink with pure natural cane sugar.
Agua mineral – Mineral water
Aguacero – Heavy rain, a downpour.
Aguado – Boring.
Aguantarse un toque – To hold on, or to wait a minute
Agüevado – Depressed or bored.
Agúevarse – To become bored.
Agüevazón - A letdown or a feeling of disappointment.
Agúizotes – Superstitious beliefs.
Ahí nos vidrios – See you later.
Ahogarse en un vaso de agua – To get worked up over nothing.
Ahorcarse – To get married.
Al ajíllo – In garlic.
Al bate – To not understand something.
Al chile – Really? Are you serious??
Al despiste – Discretely.
Al rato – Perhaps, or it could happen.
Al tiro – Immediately.
Al trole – On foot.
Alborotado – Sexually excited.
Alborotar el panal – Stir up trouble.
Alboroto – Uproar.
Aletazo – Underarm odor.
Alexandra – Ale.
Alforjas – Saddlebags, panniers.
Alguien – Someone
Alimentar las pulgas – To sleep.
Almanaques or primaveras – Refers to one's age.

Alzar con el santo y la limosna - To rob everything.
Amansar la mula – To get married.
Amarrar el pedro – Fail to pay a debt.
Amarrar el perro – To pay less than owed on a debt.
Amarrarse la enaguas – To act tough or to impose authority.
Amarrarse la gorda – To cause an uproar or start a fight.
Amarrarse los pantalones – To act tough or authoritarian.
Ametrallar – To machinegun someone.
Andar con alguien – To date someone.
Andar con el moco caído - To be sad or depressed.
Andar de mano sudada - To have a boyfriend or girlfriend.
Andar miado – To have bad luck.
Andar un ojo al cristo – To be careful
Añejo – An unkempt, dirty person.
Angelitos or niños – Criminals.
Animalada – An act caused by bad manners.
Apagado – Listless person, lethargic.
Apear las placas del carro – To revoke license plates for traffic violations.
Apenado – Embarrassed.
Aperezado – Lazy.
Apestoso - To stink.
Apiar a alguien – To knock some down.
Aplayado – Girlified, effeminate.
Apretar – To passionately kiss someone.
Aprete – A passionate kiss.
Aprobar algo con el pulgar para arriba – To give the thumbs up.
Apuntarse – To participate.
Apurado – To be in a hurry.
Arañitas – 1. Small spiders. 2. Varicose veins.
Arepa – 1. Corn pancake . Female genitalia (labia majora).
Argolla – A click of people, to have clout.
Armar un molote – To raise an uproar or to cause a scene.
Armario – Clothes closet.
Armarse la gorda – To raise an uproar, to start a fight.
Aro or llanta – Rim (tire).
Arrancado – To be mad, angry.
Arrastrada – Woman of the streets.
Arratonarse – Suffer a muscular cramp.

Arriar – To hit someone.
Arrimado – A moocher, a freeloader.
Arrugar la jacha – To frown
Aserricense – Someone from the mountain town Aserrí.
Asesino a sueldo – Hitman, a hired killer.
Así es la vida – That's life
Asomársele la pelona – To die
Ateniense – A resident from the mountain town of Atenas.
Aterro – A large amount.
Aticarse – To become Costa Rican in habits & customs
Atollarse – To get dirty.
Atracador – Someone who overcharges.
Atracar – To overcharge.
Atravesado – Crazy.
Atropellar – To run over with a car.
Aventar – To rob.
Aventón – To hitch a ride.
Avionetazo – A plane crash.
Avispado – 1. Sharp. 2. Sharp-wittted, intelligent.
Avivarse – To be up to date or on top of things.
Ayote – Stupid.
Azote – 1. A whip. 2. Someone attractive.

Bb

Babosada – Stupidity.
Baboso – Stupid.
Bailarse a la justicia - To outsmart or avoid the law.
Bajarle el humo a alguien - To put people in their place.
Bajarle el piso a alguien – To steal Someone's job.
Bajarle los humos a alguien – To discourage someone.
Bajarse los humos – To become disappointed.
Baldazo – A heavy rain.
Balear – To shoot.
Banano – 1. A banana. 2. Male sexual organ (vulgar).
Bañazo – Fool, ridiculous.
Bandido – An astute person or a rascal.
Bañera (tina) – bathtub.
Barra – A group or gang of young people.
Barra libre – A binge drinking party.
Barrer con todo – To take it all.
Batazo – A guess.
Bateador – Someone who guesses.
Batear - To lie or talk a lot of foolishness.
Batir lodo – Vehicular off-roading.
Bebé, la bebé – A baby boy or girl.
Beneficio – A plant where coffee grains are roasted.
Berrinche – A temper tantrum.
Besar – 1.To kiss. 2. To collide (Two vehicles).
Bestia – A stupid person (insult).
Bicha - A motorcycle.
Bici - Bicicleta or bicycle.
Bicicleta a la medida – A custom-built bike.
Bicicleta de montaña – A mountain bike.
Bielas – A bike's crank set.
Bien pellizcado/a - An astute person.
Birra – A beer.
Birrear – To drink beer.
Blanco - A cigarette.
Blocaje rápido – A quick release.
Boca – An appetizer, a snack.

Boca de culo de gallina – A small mouth (vulgar).
Bocado- A mouthfull or a snack.
Bochinche – A fight.
Bochinchero – A fighter.
Bocón – Someone with a big mouth (figurative).
Bola de billar – Bald (pate).
Bola de manteca – A ball of fat (heavy person).
Bolados – Advice.
Bolas – Testicles (vulgar).
Bolsear - To pick someone's pocket.
Bomba – 1. A gas station as opposed to a gasolinera. 2. A strong mixture of liquor. 3. Type of rhyme.
Bomba or inflador – Pump.
Bombazo – 1. Violent automobile crash. 2. Strong alcoholic drink.
Bombearse – To get drunk or bombed.
Bombeta – A firecracker.
Bombón – An eminently attractive woman.
Borona – A crumb.
Boronas – Bread crumbs.
Borracho – Drunk.
Bostezo – A boring person.
Botar el rancho – To vomit.
Botar el tapón - To be deceived.
Botaratas – Someone who wastes money.
Botarse – To be generous.
Bote – Jail.
Botella – Bottle.
Bracear – To stroke, swimming or swinging one's arms.
Brete – Work.
Breteador – Hard working.
Bretear – To work.
Brincar de alegría - To be happy.
Brincar en una pata - To be happy.
Brocha – Literally means brush. 2, Fellatio artist.
Brochazo – Praise.
Broncón – One big mess.
Brumoso – 1. Resident of Cartago, Costa Rica. 2. Fan of that city's football team.
Buchón – Someone selfish.

Buena carrocería – A good body/figure.
Buena chasis – A good body/figure.
Buena hablada – A good talker.
Buena nota – 1. A good grade. 2. A cool person.
Buenas – Good morning, good afternoon.
Buen Pa – The women's jail is The Buen Pastor.
Bulto – A child's book bag.
Burlar la muerte – To cheat death.
Burrada – A stupid act.
Burro/a – Someone who smuggles drugs on their body.
Buscar pelos en la sopa – To nitpick.
Busto – The bust, breasts.

Cc

¡Chúpeme el culo! – Kiss my butt
Caballada – A stupid act.
Caballos – Pants.
Cabecear – 1. To move one's head. 3. To nod off. 3. To hit a soccer ball with one's head.
Cabeza de huevo – Egghead.
Cabeza de pollo – Dumb.
Cabeza dura– A stubborn person.
Cabina – A room (in a hotel).
Cabra – Woman, girlfriend (disrespectful).
Cabreado – Mad.
Cabrearse – To become mad.
Cabro (a) – Boyfriend or girlfriend
Cabrón – A man (vulgar).
Cacharpilla or carcacha – A jalopy or an old car.
Cachetón – Fat.
Cachetonas or gorditas – King size beer bottles..
Cachos – Shoes.
Cadena – Chain, logging chain or franchise chain.
Caer – To visit, as in to drop in.
Caer en la pura picha – To dislike someone (very vulgar).
Caer en oidos sordos – To fall on deaf ears.
Caer redondo – To fall hook line and sinker.
Caerle la peseta – To understand something.
Cagadera – Diarrhea (vulgar).
Cagarse de risa – To laugh a lot (vulgar).
Cagarse en algo – To spoil something (vulgar).
Cagarse en alguien – To do something bad to someone.
Cagarse en la gran puta – To spoil something (very vulgar).
Cagarse en la leche – To ruin something (very vulgar).
Caite - Shoe.
Calzón – Woman's underwear (panties and bra).
Camanance – A dent in a car fender or body.
Cámara – tiretube.
Camarón – An odd job.
Camaroneando – To work odd jobs.

Cambiarle el agua al pajarito – To urinate (vulgar).
Cambio trasero – rear derailer on a bike.
Camisa de once varas – A bad situation.
Camote – An odd or strange person.
Campo – 1. The countryside. 2. Room or space.
Campo santo - cemetery.
Caña – a Colón (money).
Cañas – Slang for Costa Rican money instead of colones.
Candado – Lock.
Canear - To be in jail.
Cañeros – People from the town of Cañas.
Canícula – A dry period in the weather during the month of August.
Cantar – 1. Literally to sin. 2. To squeal or to snitch.
Cantar – To tell on someone, to snitch.
Cantar la gallina – The woman rules the house.
Cantar sin guitarra – To give oneself away.
Capearse – To escape or dodge something.
Carajada – Any thing or object.
Carajillo – Child
Carajo – Person.
Carambada – A thing.
Carambolar – To beat up someone.
Carbonear – To incite another person to do something.
Carbonero – Someone who incites others.
Caribarro – A shameless person.
Caripálida - A paleface.
Caripicha – Penis face (very insulting).).
Carlos – Caliche or Cali.
Carnavalear – To have a good time.
Carne de presidio - A prisoner.
Carne de tabo – Jail meat, a prisoner is worthless like cannon fodder.
Caro – Car (coche is not used._
Cartagineses – Folks from Cartago, Costa Rica.
Carterazo – To have your wallet stolen or robbed,
Cartucho – Slang for the Costa Rican city of Cartago.
Casado – A lunch or dinner plate in restaurants.
Cascarudo/a - A person without shame.
Casi se palmó – To almost die.
Casperín – like Casper the ghost (a very white person).

Catrinearse - To dress-up in good clothes.
Cejas de perico – Thick eyebrows.
Cejijunto – Eyebrows that meet.
Celu – Cell phone or mobile phone.
Celular - Cell phone.
Celulitis – 1. Cellulite. 2.An addiction to use of a cellphone.
Cerchas – Beams in the ceiling of a house.
Cero a la izquierda (un) – Someone without ability, a nobody.
Cerote – An obnoxious person (vulgar).
Cerrar el chinamo – To finish what you are doing and leave.
Cerrar el paraguas – To die.
Cerveza – Beer.
Champaña or champán – Champagne.
Chances – Lottery.
Chancho – Someone with bad table manners.
Chanchos– 1. Literally pigs. 2. Buttocks.
Chanear - To get dressed up or spruce up.
Chante – House.
Chapa – A coin or a stupid person.
Chapear – To cut the grass or brush.
Chapulín – A juvenile delinquent, gang member.
Charral – A field covered with brush.
Chavala – Girl.
Chavalo – Boy
Chayotera - Signature..
Chele – Someone with white skin.
Chema – Shirt
Chepe – A snoop.
Chepear – To snoop.
Chepito – A snoop.
Chicha – 1. Anger. 2. Alcoholic beverage brewed from fermented corn.
Chichada – a drunken party.
Chichero – A common drunk, an alcoholic.
Chichí – A baby.
Chido – Cool.
Chiflado – Crazy.
Chiflón or Ráfaga - A gust of wind or a burst of air.
Chile – A joke.

Chimenea – chimney.
Chinamo – A booth or stand on the street.
Chinche – Thumbtack.
Chinchorro – A dilapidated, old house.
Chinear – To spoil or "baby" someone.
Chinga - A cigarette butt.
Chingar – Causing harm.
Chingo – Nude.
Chingoleta – A woman wearing revealing, provocative clothes.
Chiripa – Coincidence or fluke.
Chispa – An intelligent person.
Chiva – Excellent.
Chivo – A man supported by a woman. 2. A small concert.
Chochosca – Money.
Chocobola – 1. Soccer, 2. round chocolate candy wrapped in aluminum foil and decorated to resemble a miniature soccer ball.
Chocosca - Money.
Cholo – Someone with dark skin.
Chonete – A hat.
Chopo - A handgun, pistol.
Chores – Short pants or cutoffs.
Chori – Short for chorizo, or an illegal business deal.
Choricear – To do business illegally, to fence stolen property.
Choricero – Someone who does illegal business.
Chorizo – 1. Pork sausage. 2. Penis. 3. An illegal business.
Chorreados – A type of pancake.
Chota – Making fun of something or someone
Chotas – Ridicule.
Choza or chante – House.
Chozón – A big home.
Chucear – To give someone an electric shock.
Chuchinga – Wifebeater.
Chuica – A rag or old clothes.
Chulear – To leach off someone or to swindle.
Chulo – Someone who lives off others.
Chumeco – Someone with dark skin.
Chunche – Any thing or object.
Chupahuevos – An ass kisser or servile person (vulgar).
Chupas – Lollipops.

Chuzo - Car.
Ciclovía – Bike path.
Cielo raso– Ceiling.
Cien metros – One city block (literally 100 meters).
Cien varas – One block.
Cierre Rápido – A quick release.
Clavar el pico – To fall asleep.
Clavear – To protest.
Clavo - A problem (literally a nail).
Cleta - Bicycle, derived from bicicleta.
Cletear – To ride a bicycle.
Cletero/a – A bicyclist.
Cocina – Kitchen.
Coco – A head or a shaved head.
Codear – To elbow someone.
Codearse - To hobnob, rub shoulders with, to work a room.
Codo – 1. The elbow. 2. Cheapskate.
Coger – To fornicate.
Cohete - A handgun.
Cojones – Balls (testicles).
Colado – A party crasher, someone not invited.
Cole - Colegio or high school.
Colear – To move or wag one's tail, a car fishtailing.
Colgar los tacos – To retire.
Colgar los tenis – To die
Colmillo – 1. A fang, 2. Someone astute or smart.
Colmilludo – Big eye teeth like Count Dracula.
Colocho – Curl (hair).
Color – Shame
Come mierda (un) – A bad person.
Comedor – Dining room
Comer como huérfano – To eat like an orphan or to be very hungry.
Comer como lima nueva – To eat a lot. (A lima is a sharp-toothed, raspy file).
Comer en olla grande – To have an overweight girlfriend or spouse.
Comerle a alguien – To denigrate someone.
Comerse la bronca – To be in trouble
Comerse la presa - To be stuck in traffic.
Comerse sus palabras – To eat your own words.

Comerse un gallo – To have sex (slang).
Comerse vivo a alguien – To eat Someone alive (figuratively).
Como alma que lleva el diablo – Do something fast.
Como dios lo trajo al mundo – Stark naked, birthday suit.
Como entierro de pobre – To do something expeditiously.
¿Cómo amaneció? – Good morning! How do you feel this morning?
¿Cómo está el arroz? – What is the situation?
¿Cuántos almanaques tienes? - How old are you?
Compa – Buddy, a friend.
Compañeros – Pals, buddies
Compita – A buddy, a pal. Same as compañero
Componentes – Components.
Componerse – Change one's attitude for the better.
Con el moco caído – To be sad.
Con hielo – With ice (Mixed alcoholic drink).
Con mucho gusto – You're welcome.
Con pan y queso, nadie se pone obeso – Even if you eat poorly you won't get fat.
Con permiso – Excuse me.
Con toda la pata – Great, fantastic.
Concha – 1. Sea shell 2. Pudenda, labia.
Conchada – A gross act.
Concho – A gross person.
Condenado – A smart person or rascal.
Cool – Good or great.
Copa – An alcoholic drink.
Copo – Snow cone.
Corcho – Cork.
Corona – Gears.
Correrse las tejas – To go crazy.
Corrongo – Nice or good.
Cortarle el rabo – To fire someone from their job.
Cortesía de la casa – On the house, gratis.
Corvas – Legs.
Coscorrón – To hit some on the head with your knuckles.
Costarricense - A Costa Rican.
Costroso – A dirty person.
Cotorra – Someone who talks a lot.
Crecer como la espuma – To rise like sea foam when someone

experiences success quickly.
Creerse doña toda – To be conceited.
Creerse la mamá de Trazan – To be conceited.
Cremallera – Zipper.
Cruz – Shirt.
Cruzar palabras – To cross words.
Cuadrar – To like something.
Cualquier persona – Anyone.
Cuanto cuesta? – How much does it cost?
Cuarto de baño – Bathroom.
Cuatro culos – To have a big butt (offensive).
Cuatro ojos – Four eyes, someone who wears glasses.
Cuellilargo – Having a long neck, a type of beer bottle.
Cuello de tortuga – Turtleneck.
Cuenta – Bill.
Cuentear – To gossip or to spread falsehoods.
Cuentero – A liar, a gossip.
Cuerero – Someone who consorts with ugly women.
Cuero – A woman with a bad reputation, an ugly woman.
Cuerpazo – A good body, a fine figure.
Cuerpo de almohada vieja – To have an uninspiring body.
Cuerpo de gallina – To have no hips.
Cuete - A handgun.
Cueva – 1. Cave. The nickname of Saprissa soccer stadium.
Cuidado – Careful.
Cuita – Excrement (vulgar).
Cuitear – To defecate (vulgar).
Culantro – Butt, rear end or woman (vulgar).
Culata - Riflebutt.
Culatear – To recoil, as in when a gun kicks.
Culear or culiar (vulgar)- To fornicate.
Culiolo – A male homosexual (vulgar)
Culo – Ass, vulgar word.
Culo de tres nalgas – A conceited woman.
Culo pelado – Nude (vulgar).
Cultura del guaro - Consumption of sugarcane-based liquor (guaro).
Cumiche – The youngest child, the baby of the family.
Cumple – Abbreviation for cumpleaños or birthday.
Cumplir su palabra – To keep one's word.

Dd

Dar atole con el dedo – To string someone along.
Dar bola – To flirt or pay attention to someone.
Dar cátedra - To teach someone a lesson figuratively.
Dar con el santo en tierra - To let something fall.
Dar la mano – To shake hands
Dar la palabra – To yield the floor.
¿Diay? – What can be done about it?
¿Dormiste conmigo? – Did you sleep with me? Said when someone doesn't say greet you in the morning.
Dar la talla – To do a good job.
Dar pelota – To flirt or pay attention to someone.
Dar un giro – To take turn figuratively, a life has turned around or changed completely.
Dar una lección – To teach a lesson to someone
Dar una mano – To help someone
Dar una paliza – To beat someone
Dar vuelta – To be unfaithful to one's mate.
Darle un empujón – To push someone or thing. 2. To help someone.
Darle vueltas a un asunto – To toss around an idea.
Darse por vencido– to throw in the towel or to give up.
Darse un relax – To kick back or, To relax
De buenas a primeras – Immediately.
De cabo a rabo – From beginning to end.
De feria – On top of that.
De la lagartija para arriba todo es cacería – Everything is fair game.
De la mano a la boca se pierde la sopa – Easier said than done
De los once mil diablos – Big.
De película – Excellent.
De por sí – Anyway.
De segunda mano – Second hand (a car or information).
De un pronto u otro – Suddenly.
De verdad? - Really?
De viaje – All at once.
Dedear – To move a finger.
Dedo gordo or pulgar – The thumb.

Degollar – to cut someone's throat.
Dejado – Someone with an untidy appearance.
Déjame pensarlo – Give me time to think about it.
Dejar botado a alguien – To stand up someone, to break a date
Dejar como novia del pueblo – To stand up someone.
Dejar con la palabra en la boca – to leave someone talking.
Dejar el tren – To become an old maid.
Dejar en capilla ardiente - To bother someone.
Dejar plantado – To stand up someone, to break an appointment.
Dejémonos de vainas – Seriously?
Del dicho al hecho hay mucho trecho – Talk is cheap
Del Plato a la boca se pierde la sopa – Talk is cheap
Delatar – To tell on someone, to snitch.
Deme un toque – Give me a touch, give me a second.
Dentar – Means to teeth (Toddlers).
Desafiar la muerte – To defy death.
Desahogarse - To get something off one's chest.
Desaprobar algo con el pulgar para abajo – Thumbs down.
Desayunador – A breakfast counter.
Descarado – A shameless person.
Descuatizar – To quarter someone.
Deshuesadero – A chop shop for stolen cars.
Desmadre – Total chaos.
Desnudar un santo par vestir otro - To rob Peter to pay Paul.
Despabilarse – To be on top of things.
Despachar – To kill someone.
Despelote – A mess.
Despiche – A mess, a disaster. 2. To shoot up the town.
Desviador delantero – The front derailers on a bike.
Desviadores – Derailers on a bike.
Detras del Palo – Someone who doesn't know what they're talking about (talking from behind the tree).
Devolver los peluches - To return the teddy bears and CDs when a couple breaks up.
Día del tata – Father's Day.
Dichos - Sayings.
Dientes – The teeth on a chain ring or ring gear
Dientes de ardilla – Big front teeth
Dientes de maíz – To have undersized teeth

Dientón – To have big teeth
Diezmembrar – To dismember
¡Dios guarde! – God forbid!
Disparar contra – To shoot at.
Doble, triple – Double, triple shot.
Doc - Abbrev. for doctor or doctor in English
Dolor de culo – A pain in the ass (vulgar).
Dolor de huevos – A pain in the balls or neck (vulgar).
Dolor de jupa - A headache.
Domingazo – An event scheduled on a Sunday.
Domingueño/a - A resident from Santo Domingo, Heredia.
Doña – Wife.
Dormitorio – Bedroom
Ducha – Shower
Dumbo – Big ears

Ee

Echado – Lazy.
Echar – To kiss.
Echar adelante y arar con los bueyes que tenemos – To persevere.
Echar al agua – To tell on someone, to snitch.
Echar el caballo – To flirt in an attempted seduction.
Echar el cuento – To say nice things to seduce someone.
Echar el ruco - To make a pass, to flirt, to proposition;
Echar la casa por la ventana – To spend lavishly
Echar para el saco – To chalk up something to experience.
Echar patas – 1. To sprout feet. 2. When things disappear (theft).
Echar un lance – To conquer a woman.
Echarse el equipo al hombro – To carry a team on one's back.
Echarse flores – To praise oneself.
Echarse la soga al cuello – To get married.
Echarse un pedo – To fart, to pass gas (vulgar).
Eje – An axle shaft.
Elena – a small person.
Embarcar – To put someone in a jam. To involve them in something.
Embutido – Sausage, slang for shady business dealings.
Empuchado/a - A diligent or hard working person
Empuncharse – To make a big effort.
En bocas cerradas no entran moscas – It is best to keep quiet.
En dos patadas – In a jiffy.
En dos taconazos – In a jiffy.
En las rocas – On the rocks (Mixed alcoholic drink).
En puta – A lot of something (vulgar).
En un dos por tres – Quickly.
Enano – A short person or a child.
Enchompiparse – To get mad.
Enchorpar – To put in jail.
Enculado – In love (vulgar).
Enemigo – Enemy.
Enfiebrado – Enthused.
Engañar – To joke or have fun.
Enganche – Influence.
Engavetar – To incarcereate, to put in jail.

Engomado – To have a hangover.
Enjachar una cara – To make a face at someone.
Enjachar – To stare at or to make a face at someone.
Enjaranarse – To go into debt.
Ennoviado – To have a boyfriend or girlfriend.
Enpalomar - To put in jail (Encarcelar).
Entender ni papa - To not be able to understand a single word.
Entrar con toda la valija – To be deceived by someone.
Eres lo que comes – You are what you eat.
Es de morirse – It's to die for.
Escalera – Stairs.
Escopetar – To shotgun.
Escuchar las arpas celestiales – To be close to death
Escupe fuego – Gun.
Escusado – Toilet.
Esforzarse – To make a big effort.
Esguince – A sprain.
Eslabón – The links on a chain.
Espaciadores – Spacers.
Espantoso – An ugly person or thing.
Espíritu Santo: Holy Spirit, Holy Ghost.
Esquinera – An easy woman or one with a bad reputation.
Está bien – It's ok.
Está legal – It's o.k. or cool.
Esta mamando - You are sucking, you are failing.
Estaca – A cheapskate.
Estamos tablas – We are even (debt)!
Estañón sin fondo – A glutton or a bottomless pit
Estar a las puertas de la muerte – To be at death's doors
Estar a mano – To be even (you no longer owe anything).
Estar a puro té de tilo - To be nervous.
Estar añejo/a – To need a bath.
Estar bajo el poder de uno or tener poder sobre uno – To be under one's thumb.
Estar bien parado – To have it made.
Estar cagado – To have bad luck (vulgar).
Estar cagado en plata – To have a lot of money.
Estar como agua para chocolate – To be boiling mad.
Estar como chaqueta de salonero – To be broke.

Estar como hormiga en popi – To be happy.
Estar como paco – good enough to eat or devour.
Estar como todos los diablos – To be mad.
Estar con el moco caído – To be down or depressed.
Estar con toda la pata – Great.
Estar con una pata en la tumba – To have one foot in the grave.
Estar de buenas pulgas – To be in a good mood.
Estar de chicha – To be in a bad mood, grumpy.
Estar de goma – To have a hangover.
Estar de malas pulgas – To be in a bad mood.
Estar de manteles largos - To celebrate one's birthday
Estar de vaca gordas - Fat years, boom years or prosperous times.
Estar en alas de cucaracha – To be about to be fired from a job or end an relationship.
Estar en sus manos – It is up to you or in your hands
Estar en todas – To be well informed or on top of everything.
Estar en un apuro – To be in a jam or in trouble.
Estar frito – To not have a chance.
Estar fuleado – To be full.
Estar full – To be full
Estar harto/a de - To be fed up with someone or something.
Estar hasta el copete – To be fed-up with something.
Estar hasta el culo – To be drunk on your ass (vulgar).
Estar hasta el rabo – To be drunk
Estar hasta la coronilla – To be fed up with something.
Estar hasta la mecha – To be drunk.
Estar hasta la picha – Also to be very drunk (vulgar).
Estar hecho leña – To be sick, frustrated, or unmotivated.
Estar limpio – To be broke.
Estar más allá que acá – To be more dead than alive.
Estar más limpio que chaqueta de salonero – To be broke
Estar muy mami - A sexy, attractive woman.
Estar ojo al cristo – An admonition to stay alert.
Estar puras tejas – Another way to say pura vida.
Estar puros dieces – To feel great. (to be at pure tens).
Estar que se lo lleva puta – To be angry (vulgar).
Estar solo – To be unique or to be crazy.
Estar vivo y coleando – To be alive and kicking.
¡Estoy varado! – I'm stuck some place!

Estirar la pata – To die.
Estrangular – To strangle.
Estuche – A soccer stadium.
Excavar su propia tumba – To dig one's own grave.
Exito – A hit film, something successful.

Ff

Facha – Poorly dressed.
Faja – 1, A belt. 2. Fanbelt for car or truck motor.
La faja de tiros – 1. Teeth. 2. A cartridge belt for bullets.
Fajarse – To work or to study a lot.
Faltarle a uno un tornillo – To have a screw loose, to be crazy.
Farandutica – Costa Rican jet setters.
Farmacha – A bleach blonde.
Feliz como lombriz - Very happy.
Feto – An ugly person.
Fibra de carbono – Carbon fiber used in lightweight bike frames.
Fiebre – A sports fan or a fanatic.
Fiesta a todo mecate - A good party or event.
Fila – A line people wait in.
Filazo – A stabbing.
Filo – Hunger.
Filoso – 1. Sharp 2. Hungry.
Finca – A ranch, farm.
Finde – Abbreviation for weekend or fin de semana.
Fisgonear - To snoop.
Fondillo – Someone's behind.
Forrado – To have lots of money.
Forro – A cheat sheet for an exam.
Fósforo – A skinny person, skinny like a matchstick.
Fregadero – A kitchen sink.
Fregado – Sick, broken or screwed up.
Fregar – To bother.
Fregón – Someone who bothers people a lot.
Frenos – Brakes.
Frentón – Having a big forehead.
Fresco – A nervy or shameless person. 2. Cool, as in air temperature.
Fresco (refresco) – A cold, non-alcoholic drink
Fresco natural – A natural fruit or powered drink.
Fría – A beer, a cold one.
Fuera de onda – Someone not up to date on music, fashion.
Fulminar – To kill
Fumigar – To fumigate, to end a relationship or to murder.
Fut – Abbreviation for fútbol, or soccer, as they say in the EEUU.

Gg

Gabacha – A white lab coat like doctors wear.
Gacilla – A safety pin.
Gajo – An old thing or piece of junk.
Gallo – Means rooster, also spit with phlegm and mucus.
Gallo pinto – Rice and beans.
Ganar – To rob.
Ganar la vida - To earn a living.
Ganarse los frijoles - To earn a living.
Garabato – Scribbling.
Garaje (cochera) – Garage.
Garrotazos – 1. Price increases. 2. To get clubbed on the head.
Garrote – Club or big penis
Garrotear – To beat with a stick.
Gaseosa – Soft drink (carbonated soda).
Gastar a manos llenas - To be free spending.
Gastar polvo en zopilotes – To waste time on trivial matters.
Gastar saliva – To waste one's breath.
Gata – A jack to lift a car.
Gatillero – A triggerman or killer.
Gato – Someone with blue or green eyes.
Gato encerrado – More than meets the eye.
Gente – The people.
Gluteos – The gluteus maximus muscle, the buttocks.
Gogrin – Gringo. Ticos like to play with words and talk backwards.
Goma – 1. Glue 2. Hangover.
Gomón – A bad hangover.
Greña – Unkept hair.
Grifo– Faucet.
Gringada - All gringos collectively or a typical gringo behaviour.
Gringo de nacimiento, tico de corazón – Gringo by birth, tico at heart.
Gringolandia - the United States.
Gringorricense – A gringo/tico.
Gringuera – A latina who likes to spend time with gringo men.
Gringuerío - A group of gringos.
Gua Gua – Dog.

Guaca – Money.
¡Guacala! – Used to express disgust.
Guachear – To spy, watch or observe.
Guachos – Sunglasses.
Guada – Abbreviation for San José's suburb of Guadalupe.
Guamazo – A strong blow, hit or collision.
Guamazo – A violent automobile crash.
Guanaco – A disparaging term for somone from Guanacaste.
Guardabarros – Fender.
Guarera - A drunken spree.
Guaro – Moonshine (illegal liquor).
Guata – Water.
Guate - Abbrev. for Guatemala.
Guato – Dog.
Güeiso – Something bad.
Guerra santa – A holy war.
Güeval – A large amount of something.
Güevazo – A big hit or blow (vulgar).
Güevo – A lot of money.
Güevón – A man (spoken man to man).
Güevonada – A stupid act.
Güila – A little boy or girl.
Guillermo – Memo.
Güilón (un) – A beautiful young woman.
Guindado – Uninvited person or pest.
Guindo – A cliff or ravine.
Guineo, banano, mariposa, flor – A homosexual (insult).

Hh

Habladera – An habladera does a lot of talking.
Hablar (hasta) por los codos - To talk too much.
Hablar como lora hambrienta - To gab like a hungry parrot.
Hablar en chino – To not understand.
Hablar hasta por el hueco del culo - To speak out your ass.
Hablar mierda – To talk shit (vulgar).
Hablar no cuesta nada – Talk is cheap.
Hablar paja - Talk of trivial matters or B.S.
Hablar por hablar – To talk merely for the sake of it
Hablar por los codos – To talk one's head off.
Hacer el muerto – To play dead, or act like one is dead.
Hacer ojos – To flirt, to make eyes at someone.
Hacer pichuelos – To do odd jobs.
Hacer trillo – To make a name for oneself.
Hacer un McGyver – To improvise and adopt.
Hacer una cara - To make a face at someone.
Hacer una colecta – To pass the hat, to take up a collection (money).
Hacerle cabeza - To think.
Hacerle la cruz – To exclude or to not do something.
Hacerse bolas - To get confused (Confundirse).
Hacerse el mae – To play dumb.
Hacerse el ruso – To play dumb.
Hacerse humo – To disappear, literally to turn into smoke.
Hacerse punta – To get a haircut.
Hágame el favor! – Give me a break!
Hale – On business doors it means pull, also get out!
Harina – 1. Flour. 2. Money.
Hasta el copete – To be fed up with someone or something.
Hasta el culo/hasta las tetas/hasta la picha - Vulgar way to say drunk.
Hasta el rabo – Drunk.
Hasta la coronilla/el copete - To be fed up with something.
Hasta la mecha – Drunk.
Hay campo? – Is there room (space)?
Hay paso? – Is there passage, can I get through?
Hecho a mano – Handmade.
Hecho leña – To be in bad shape.

Hecho mierda – To be in bad shape (vulgar).
Hecho pistola – To be in bad shape.
Hediondo - To stink.
Hediondo – A jerk or asshole (vulgar).
Hembra – A woman (disrespectful).
Hembrón – A pretty woman.
Herma - Brother or hermano.
Hierba santa- Mint (herb).
High (la) - The upper crust or class.
Hijo de papi/papá - A spoiled rich kid.
¡Hijueputa! – Son of a bitch.
¡Huelepedos! – A kiss ass.
Hijo de puta o hijueputa – SOB.
Hijueputear -To scare or use foul language.
Hocicón – Big mouth (disrespectful).
Hociconear – To brag. (From the hocicón, an animal's snout or an insulting name for one's mouth).
Hogar (home) ducle hogar – home sweet home.
Hojear un libro – To thumb through a book.
Hombre de palabra – A man of his word.
Hombrear – To shoulder a burden.
Hombro - Shoulder.
Hongos – Mushrooms (also fungus).
Hora santa - Prayer recited before the Eucharist, or in commemoration of the suffering of Jesus Christ.
Horqueta – Fork of a bike.
Hospi - Abbrev. for hospital.
Huaca - Money.
Huaquero - Thief who robs artifacts from Indian graves.
Hueco del culo – Anus in Costa Rican Spanish (vulgar).
Huelepedos – An ass-kisser or servile person (vulgar).
Hueso – 1. A cheapskate. 2. Bone.
Huevón – A man (vulgar).
Huevos – 1. Eggs. 2. Money. 3. Balls (testicles). Tener huevos means to have balls/cojones.
Huevos de agua – Describes a man who can only father girls (vulgar).

Ii

¿Idiay? – What is the problem?
Ingenio – A plant where sugar is processed.
Inodoro - Toilet.
Irse de pollo - To do something stupid, to be made a fool of.
Irse de shopping – To go shopping.
Irse por mal camino – To go down the wrong path.
Írsele arriba a alguien – To get an advantage over someone.

Jj

¡Jale! – Hurry up! or Get moving! Boque is also used.
¡Jueputal! – Damn! (vulgar).
Jacha – Face.
Jaibo – Stupid person (insult).
Jalado – Dissipated or pale.
Jalar – To date Someone. It also means to go somewhere.
Jalar las orejas - To scold someone.
Jalarle las orejas – To pull someone's ears or to scold.
Jalarse un enjache – To make a face at someone.
Jalarse una torta – To commit an error or get pregnant.
Jalonazo - A strong electrical shock.
Jama – Food.
Jamar – To eat.
Jamonear – To bully someone.
Jamonero – Bully.
Jarana – A debt.
Jareta – Zipper.
Jarro – Face.
Jartar – To eat.
Jaus – Slang for house or casa.
Jerez – Sherry.
Jeta – Mouth.
Jetas – Liar.
Jetear – To talk a lot of crap.
Jetón – Liar.
Jetonear – To lie.
Jocote – 1. A local fruit. 2. Big toe.
Jocotear – To bother someone.
Jodedera – Incessant bothering of someone (vulgar)
Joder – To bother (vulgar form).
Jodido – Difficult, sick, broken, a stubborn or evil person (vulgar).
La Joya – Costa Rica's National Stadium
Jueeeeee...puta! - Damn! Expression of frustration (hijo de puta).
Jugado – An experienced or streetwise person.
Jugar de vivo – Brag or act cool
Jugarsela - To manage or make do.

Jumas - Drunk
Jumo – Drunk, a synonym for tapis or borracho.
Juntado – Shacked up or living with someone.
Juntos y no revueltos – To be with someone platonically .
Jupa - Someone's head
Jupa de agua - A flash flood.
Jupa de teflón – A forgetful person.
Jupón or jupona – A stubborn person.

Ll

Lacra – A thief
Lágrima – A teardrop. 2. Boulder
Lamebotas - An ass kisser, suck up, or brownoser.
Lameculos - An ass kisser, suck up or brownoser (vulgar).
Lance – A sexual conquest.
Lancha – A ferry boat.
Lanta ponchada – A flat tire.
Lapicero – A ballpoint pen.
Larguirucho – A lanky person.
Las palabras sobran y los hechos hablan – Talk is cheap.
Las paredes oyen – The walls have ears.
Las paredes tienen oídos – The walls have ears.
Las pelis – the movies.
Las tres letras - OIJ - CR's criminal investigation organization.
Lata – 1. An old bus. 2. Someone who is a nuisance
Lava huevos – Wash the eggs, the act of sucking up.
Lavabo – Bathroom sink.
Lavamanos – Bathroom sink.
Leche – 1. Milk. 2. Semen
Lecheros – Those who live in Coronado (Coro).
Leda – Age.
Legal – Acceptable.
¿Legal? – Seriously?
Leñazo - A violent automobile crash.
Leñazo - A strong blow.
Lengua santa - The Hebrew language.
Lengüetear – To lick, or stick out one's tongue.
Leva – Jacket.
Levantarle la mano a alguien – To hit someone.
Levantarse de la tumba – To rise up from the grave.
Levantín – When a bull lifts up and throws a bullfighter.
Libro manoseado – A well thumbed (much read) book.
Licor – Liquor
Liguista envenenado – Fanatical football (soccer) fan from Alajuela.
Limón – Lemon
Limpiar - To impress someone with your talent.

Limpio – Broke.
Linchar – To lynch
Liquidar – To liquidate or to kill someone.
Llamar a Hugo – To vomit.
Llanta – A spare tire around the waist.
Llave de rana – A lug wrench for a car tire.
Llegar a mis manos – To get one's hands on.
Llegar y besar el santo - To succeed at something on the first try.
Llena – A flood associated with the full moon.
Llenazo - An event lots of people attended, a raving success.
Llevarla suave – To take it easy.
Llevarse puta – To get upset (vulgar).
Llorar a moco tendido – To cry a lot.
¡Lo duda! – You said it! You are right!
Lo or la fueron - To have fired someone from their job.
Lo prometido es deuda – To have to keep a promise.
Lo que no mata, engorda – What won't kill you, only makes you fat.
Lo que sea – Whatever.
Lo tiene furris or lo tiene feo – A bad experience.
Lógica retorcida – Twisted logic.
Looser – A loser, un perdedor.
Los cuatro por cuatro – Glasses.
Los hechos distorcionados – Twisted, distorted facts.

Mm

Macha - A blonde female, usually a foreigner
Machete – 1. A machete blade. 2. One's tool of the trade.
Macho – Someone with blond hair.
Macuco – A strong person
Madre – Terrible.
Madrear – To insult someone (vulgar).
Madrear - To beat up someone.
Maduro – Male sex organ (vulgar)
Mae – Man, Woman or any person.
Maicero – A hick or country person (insult).
Maicucha – Marijuana.
Maje - Literally dummy, figuratively buddy. A term of endearment.
Majijo – Someone disfigured with a hair lip.
Mal de patria – Homesick.
Mala fama – A bad reputation.
Mala ficha – A bad reputation.
Maleta – 1. Suitcase. 2. Male genitals.
Mall – Mall. Centro Comercial.
Mamacita – A beautiful woman (vulgar).
Mamar – To flunk a test.
Mameyazo – A big blow or hit
Mami - Mother, one's wife, lover or a beautiful woman.
Mamulón – An adult or big person.
Mamulón – An immature adult who acts like a kid.
Mañas – Bad habits.
Manda huevo – I cannot believe it, or it is inconceivable.
¡Mae! – A young man or stupid person.
¡Malparido! – Bastard.
¡Mamapichas! – Someone who performs felattio.
¡Manda güevo! – It's unbelievable (vulgar). How can it be?
¡Manos a la obra¡ – Let's get to work!
¡Manos quietas! – Hands off!
Mandamás – The boss.
Manigordo – An ocelot
Mano de cartas – A hand of cards.
Mano de santo- A fast and complete cure for an ailment .

Mano derecha – A right–hand man (helper)
Mano suelta – An overly-generous person.
Manosear – To fondle.
Mantudo – A large, colorful, traditional mask
Manubrios or guías – A bike's handle bars
Manudo – A resident of the city of Alajuela.
Marco or cuadro – A frame.
María – Taximeter.
Maricón – Coward. Gay.
Mariconada – Cowardly.
Marimba – Teeth.
Más humilde que un pinto sin frijol – To be humble
Más pa'cá – Closer (contraction of más para acá).
Más para allá – Farther (away).
Más peligroso que un rifle chocho - To be very dangerous.
Más tico que el agua dulce - To be typically Costa Rican
Más tico que el gallo pinto - To be typically Costa Rican
Más tico que la maña de pedir fiado - To be typically Costa Rican.
Más tieso que un cocodrilo enyesado - Stiffer than a crocodile coated with plaster.
Más tieso que un pan de tres diás – Stiffer than a three-day-old bread.
Más torcido que cola de chancho – More twisted than a pig's tail. 2. To be unlucky.
Más vale tonto callado, que tonto hablando – A dumb person should keep quiet.
Matadero – One of Costa Rica's famous love motels.
Matalances – 1. Party pooper. 2. A kill joy.
Matar – To kill
Matar a golpes – To beat to death.
Matar a pedradas To stone to death.
Matar a tiros – To shoot to death.
Matar la culebra – To waste time.
Matón – A bully.
Me caye bien – I like you.
Me contó un pájaro – By word of mouth.
Me lleva puta – To be angry (vulgar).
Me presta una teja? - Lend me a buck?
Mear fuera del tarro – Not know what you're talking about.
Mecedora – A rocking chair.

Mecha – Marijuana.
Meche – Abbrev. for Mercedes (woman's name). 2. Mercedes Benz.
Mechudo – Person with uncombed hair.
Meco – A punch with a clenched fist.
Medalla – A 50 Colón coin.
Media naranja - Your better half, or lover.
Media teja – 500 colones (Costa Rican money).
Medio lado – Sideways.
Medir sus palabras – To carefully choose one's words.
Mejenga – Informal pick up game of soccer.
Mejenguear – To play an informal game of soccer.
Melonazos - A million dollars or a million colones.
Melos – Abbrev. for gemelos (twins).
Mentar la madre – To insult someone's mother.
Merula - A woman's makeup.
Meter el hombro – To help someone.
Meter la pata – To put your foot in your mouth.
Meter las narices en lo que no te importa – To intrude in someone's else's business.
Meter yucas - To tell lies.
Metiche – A snoopy or nosy person.
Mi amor – My love .
Mi casa es su casa – My house is your house"
Miar – To urinate (vulgar).
Mico – Female organ (vulgar).
Mientes con los dientes – To lie through one's teeth.
Mientras en mi casa estoy, rey me soy – A man's house is his castle.
Mierdoso – A brat.
Migas/migajas – Bread crumbs.
Mirar las uñas – To twiddle one's thumbs.
Molote – A crowd of people.
Momia – An ugly person.
Moncha – Hunger.
Monchar – To eat or munch.
Montar en bicicleta – to ride a bicycle.
Montarse en la carreta – To get drunk.
Monte – Marijuana.
Mop – 1. A friend or man. 2. A muppet.
Morado – A Sarprissa soccer fan.

Mordiscos - Drag racing cars
Morir a manos de – To die at the hands of.
Morir al pie del cañon – To die with your boots on.
Morir en el intento – To die trying to do something.
Morirse de frío – To be dying of the cold (figurative).
Morirse de ganas por + verb – To be dying to do something.
Morirse de hambre – To be dying of hunger, literally and figuratively.
Morirse de risa – To laugh like crazy.
Morirse de vergüenza – To die of shame.
Morirse por ... - To die for something, like a good meal.
Mosca - Money.
Mota – Marjuana.
Mover el esqueleto – To move your skeleton, to dance.
Muchacho, muchacha - Young boy or young girl
Mucho gusto - With much pleasure..
Mucho rin rin y nada de helados – All talk.
Muerto de hambre – A poor person (condescending).
Mujerear - To chase women.
Muni - Abreviation for a municipalidad or municipality.
Muppet – Friend.
Muro, tapia – Outside wall.

Nn

¡Ni a putas! – Not for anything in this world (vulgar).
¡Ni modo! – Cannot do anything about it.
¡No jodás! – Leave me alone! Stop bothering me (vulgar)!
¡No se monte! – Don't mess with me!
¡No te atraso! – I don't care what you do!
Nacer por el culo – To be ugly (very vulgar and offensive)
Nachas – The buttocks. NOT to be confused with Mexican nachos.
Nada que ver! - Nothing to see, no big deal.
Nadadora – As flat as a board (insulting).
Nadie – Nobody.
Nalgas – The buttocks.
Nalguear – To spank.
Naranjeños – Residents of the town of Naranjo.
Narizón – A big nose.
Nave - Car.
Necio/a – A stubborn person.
Ni mierda – Nothing (vulgar).
Ni papa – Nothing.
Ni un cinco – Broke.
Nica - Abbrreviation for a Nicaragüense (Nicaraguan).
No dar el brazo a tocer – To not give in when arguing.
No entrarle ni una bala – To be so full after eating that there is not even room for a bullet in your body.
No es el santo de mi devoció - Not my cup of tea.
No es jugando – It is not a joke.
No es la ropa, es la percha – It's not the clothes but what's underneath.
No estar en nada – To be in the dark or to know nothing.
No importa – It's not important doesn't matter
No joda!/no jodás! - Don't bother me! Leave me alone!
No me digas! – Don't tell me! No way!
No se le quita lo gringo ni banándose - Always be gringo no matter what else you do.
No se monte! - Don't mess with me!
No tener pelos en la lengua – To speak one's mind

36

No tener un pelo de tonto – To not be dumb.
Nombrar a dedo - To handpick someone for a task.
Norteño - A gringo.
Nota – A good thing.
Novio, novia – Boyfriend or girlfriend
Novios – Sweethearts, or the bride and groom.

Oo

Ofe - Feo (ugly) said backwards.
Ofis – Police officers
Oídos tísicos – To have big ears.
Oijoto - OIJ - CR's criminal investigation organization.
Ojear – To stare. Not to be confused with hojear - to leaf through a book.
Ojo! – Watch out!
Ojos soñolientos – Sleepy eyes.
Olla de carne – Dish made of meat and vegetables.
Orejón – Big ears.
Orinar fuera del tarro – To not know what you're talking about.
Otra vuelta, otra ronda – Another round of drinks

Pp

Pachanga – A party or blast.
Pachuco – 1. Someone with unacceptable social customs. 2. Women's underwear. 3. Street slang used by young people.
Paco – A policeman (insult).
Paganini – Someone generous who always pays or picks up the bill.
Paja – Lies or B.S.
Pajoso – Someone who speaks a lot of paja or B.S.
Palabrear – To try and convince someone.
Palabrota – A swear word.
Palanca – Pull or influence.
Palanca de freno – Brake arm.
Palenque – A thatched hut.
Paleta– Lollipop.
Palmarse – To die.
Palmear – To pat or clap.
Palo – A tree.
Palo de piso – A mop.
Pan comido – Something that is very easy to accomplish.
Pan duro es mejor que ninguno – Beggars can't be choosers.
Pana -Abbrev. for Panameño or Panamanian.
Pancho – Female organ (vulgar).
Pancista – He who always roots for the winning soccer team.
Pandiller – Motorcyclist dressed like a Hells Angel, only harmless.
Panga – A small motorboat
Paño – A bath towel.
Panocha – Female genital organ.
Panta – Surfing shorts
Pantaloneta – Shorts
Panza birrera – A beer belly
Panza cervecera – Also, a beer belly
Panza llena, corzón contento – If you are full, you are happy.
Panzona – Pregnant.
Paperos - Cartagineses (Resident of Cartago), called potato people because they cultivate potatoes.
Papi – 1. A term of endearment for a husband, or boyfriend. 2. A young person with money who dresses well.

Papucho – Good looking man.
Papudo/a – To have lots of money (adinerado).
Paque – Secondhand.
Paquetear – To deceive
Para llevar – To carry-out (food).
Paracaidas – A party crasher.
Pararle la peluca a alguien – To make someone mad, upset.
Pararse de uñas - To get upset.
Parecer un bistec de 5 pesos solo nervios - To be nervous.
Pared – An inside wall.
Parientes – Relatives
Parlanchín - Someone who talks incessantly.
Parpadear – To blink or flicker the eyes.
Parqueo de bicicletas – Bike racks or place to park a bike.
Parte – A traffic or parking ticket.
Partir la espalda – To break one's back by working too hard.
Pasar el sombrero - To pass the hat to collect donations.
Pasar la tijera – To cut a budget like government.
Pasar raspando – To just scrape by on a test/exam.
Pase – Bus fare.
Pasillo – Hallway.
Patas de mono – To have flat feet like a monkey.
Patas de yuca – Someone with very white skin on their feet.
Patear – To kick.
Patear con los dos – Bisexual (vulgar).
Patear el balde – To kick the bucket, to die.
Patinetero - A skateboarder.
Patio – Back yard.
Pato de la fiesta or el hazmereir – A laughingstock.
Patriarca – Foot (body part).
Paveño – A resident of the San José suburb of Pavas.
Pecho de zapo – A big chest.
Pechonalidad – Personality.
Pechuga – The breast of a chicken, or a woman's breast.
Pedalear – To pedal a bike.
Pedales – Bike pedals.
Pedir un ride – To thumb a ride or hitchhike.
Pega - A pain in the neck, indigestion, anything impeding progress.
Pega de chorizo – Something useless.

Pegar el gordo – To win the lottery.
Pegarse una ruleada – To sleep.
Pelada de culo - A screw up (vulgar).
Pelagatos - A useless or insignificant person
Pelar el ojo - An admonition to be alert!
Pelar los dientes – To smile.
Pelarse el culo – To commit an error or to make a fool of oneself.
Peli - A movie. Abbrev. for película.
Pellejo – An unattractive woman (insult).
Pellizcado – A smart person.
Pelona – The angel of death or Grim Reaper.
¡Pelo el ojo! – Watch out!
¡Póngale! – Hurry up!
¡Pura vara! – Lies!
¡Pura vida! – Great or fantastic.
Pelo de elote – Unattractive hair.
Pelo de gato – Drizzle, light, soft rain.
Pelón – A party.
Pelona - Death like the Grim Reaper or the Angel of Death.
Pelota de gente – A large group of people.
Pelotearse – To gather with friends.
Pendejada – Something of little importance.
Peni - Abbrev. for penitenciaría (penitentiary).
Pepa – Female sex organ (vulgar).
Pepiado – In love.
Pepiarse – To fall in love.
Pepita – Female sex organ (vulgar).
Peque – A hit film, something successful (Exito).
Peques – Children.
Perder hasta la casa santa – To lose everything.
Perder un tornillo – To be missing a screw, crazy.
Perdón – Said when bumping into someone.
Perico - Cocaine's sharp pain like a parrot biting your nose.
Perico – Parrot.
Perra – A loose woman (vulgar).
Perrear – To chase women (vulgar).
Perro – A girl-crazy man.
Perro amarrado – A tied dog, to be in debt.
Perro que come huevos, ni quemándole el hocico – 1. Hard to

change. 2. Someone's negative behavior.
Perro que ladra no muerde – Someone's bark is worse than his bite.
Pesado – Obnoxious.
Pescuezo – Neck (body part).
Peso – One colón (Costa Rican Money).
Pestañear – to wink or blink or flutter one's eyelashes.
Picar – To drag race.
Picha – A vulgar term for the penis. (vulgar).
Pichacear - To beat someone up (vulgar).
Pichazal – A large quantity.
Pichel – Face or glass pitcher.
Pichinga – A large receptacle used to storw liquid.
Pichudo – Nice.
Pichuleo - An odd job.
Pick-up – A pick-up truck.
Picón – 1. A drag racer. 2. Someone who picks at their food.
Piedra – Crack cocaine.
Piedrero – Crack head (cocaine).
Pierna – Someone of influence.
Pijarse – To get high on marijuana.
Piñazo – A violent blow or collision.
Pinche – Tight, stingy.
Pinga – Male sex organ (vulgar).
Pingüino – A nun dressed in her habit (penguin bad taste).
Piñones – Sprocket.
Pinta – A delinquent.
Pinta – Appearance.
Pinto – Rice and beans.
Pipa - Pipe used to smoke weed.
Pipa – 1. A smart person 2. Cold coconut drinks sold at the beach.
Piques - Drag racing cars.
Piropos - Catcalls shouted out to women walking down the street.
Pisar – To have sexual relations (vulgar).
Piso – Floor level, first floor, second et cetera).
Pistol – 1. Pistol (firearm). 2. Penis.
Pito – Literally a whistle and not particularly offensive.
Planchar la oreja – Sleep.
Planta baja – The ground floor
Platanazo – A homosexual (vulgar).

Plátano – A male homosexual (vulgar).
Plato – chain ring.
Playa – A female homosexual.
Playada – 1. Feminine behavior or a bad experience. 2. Treason.
Plumero - A duster.
Plumero –Someone with wild unruly hair.
Polaco – A Jewish person.
Polaquear – To sell from door to door.
Poli - Abbrev. for policía or police.
Policletos – Police riding bicycles.
Pollo – 1. A novice, someone inexperienced. 2. A beautiful woman.
Polo – Someone out of style. A country bumpkin or a hick.
Polvazal -A lot of dust.
Polvazo – Someone who is good in bed (vulgar).
Polvo – Sex act (vulgar).
Pomada de canario – A cure-all used in back in the day.
Poner a uno al día – To bring someone up-to-date.
Poner como un Chuica – To humiliate.
Ponerle bonito – To do something well.
Ponerle camisa de madera – 1. To put a wooden shirt on someone. 2. To put in a coffin, or to kill.
Ponerle candela or ponerle bonito – To make an effort, to try hard.
Ponerlo – To have sex (woman).
Ponerse águila – Pay attention.
Ponerse al hilo – Pay your bills to date.
Ponerse bravo – To get mad.
Ponerse chivo – To get mad.
Ponerse chúcaro - To become very angry.
Ponerse de todos colores – To become embarrassed.
Ponerse full – to be full like a soccer stadium.
Ponerse tapis – To get drunk.
Póngale – Hurry up!
Por dicha – Fortunately.
Por fa – Abbrev. for por favor, or please.
Por la boca muere el pes – be careful what you say
Por otras bocas – By word of mouth.
Por si moscas – Just in case.
Por un pelo no es mono – To be very hairy, hirsute.
Por una baba no es mono – To be very hairy, hirsute.

Porta a mí – Who cares?
Porta bicicleta – A bike rack for a car.
Portaequipaje – A rack on the back of a bike
Portal – Porch.
Portrero – Pasture.
Poste de manubrio – A handle bar stem/post.
Poza – Swimming hole.
Precarista – A squatter.
Premiada – Pregnant.
Presa – A traffic jam.
Presi - Abbrev. for president
Princesos – Pampered, pretty boy, soccer players.
Pringar – To splatter.
Profe - A teacher
Prosti - Short for prostituta or prostitute.
Pulpería – A small corner grocery store.
Pulseador – 1. A hard worker. 2. An arm wrestler.
Pulseándola – Working hard.
Pulsear – To bargain or to work hard.
Puño – Handlebar grip
Pura carnita – When something is good.
Pura gozadera – Enjoyment, fun.
Pura mierda – Full of crap! (vulgar).
Pura Paja – 1. Straw. 2. Pure lies.
Pura vara! - Lies!
Pura vida – A happy, pure life, all is well.
Puras tejas – 1. Pure Texas. 2.Great.
Puris – Abbrev. for the mountain town Puriscal
Puros cienes - Great!
Puros dieces - Very well.
Pussy – Stupid, ugly or nice. Depending on context.
Puta – Whore (vulgar).
Putada – A thing (vulgar).
Putero – A whore house (vulgar).
Putica – A Costa Rica whole (vulgar).

Qq

¿Qué es la vara? – How's it going?
¿Qué me dice? – How's it going?
¡Qué ahuevado! – How boring!
¡Qué bostezo! How boring!
¡Qué cáscara! – What nerve!
¡Qué chiva! – How cool or neat!
¡Qué color! - How embarrassing!
¡Qué dicha! – Good!
¡Qué grossy! – How gross!
¡Qué guabal! – What a lie, or what luck!
¡Qué heidy! – What a lie!
¡Qué madre! – What a drag!
¡Qué mica! – How bad or awful!
¡Qué pelada! – How embarrassing!
¡Qué pereza! – What a drag!
¡Qué ricas nalgas! What a nice butt you have!
¡Qué rico! – How good! (referring to food, woman)
¡Qué rollo! – What a pity!
¡Qué tirada! – What a problem, pity!
¡Qué torta! – What a mess!
¡Qué va! – No way!
Que Asco – Gross.
Que camote – What a yam, what craziness.
Que despiche! - What a mess! or What a good time!
Qué dicha! – What splendid luck! or fantastic!
Que es la vara? - What's the deal?
Que Lechero – What a milkman, somebody very lucky.
Que m'iche? - What's up?
Que mala nota! - What a bad person!
Qué me dice? - What do you say? or Tell me what's up?
Que pega - What a stick. Someone, or something, annoying.
Que pelada – What a peeled, to do something embarrassing.
Que pereza! - Ugh, what a drag!
Que quería, galleta María? - What do you want, a cookie?
Que tigra – What a female tiger, bored, feeling lethargic.

Que tigra ir a bretiar hoy – I feel too lazy to go to work.
Que tigra me tengo - I am so, so bored.
Que torta – What a patty, which is to say, to make a mistake.
Que vacilón! - How fun!
Quebrada – A stream or brook.
Quedado – Someone who flunks the school year.
Quedar como jarro de loco – To be in bad shape
Quedar como perro de cura – To be full after a meal.
Quedar como un ajillo – To be very white or clean
Quedar como un culo – Look like a fool (vulgar).
Quedar hecho una melcocha – Twisted wreckage, a car accident.
Quedarse – To flunk school.
Quedarse como misa – To be silent.
Quedarse en la calle – To go broke.
Quedarse para vestir santos - To remain unmarried (woman).
Quemar callos - To burn callouses, to dance.
Quemar hule – To burn rubber (tires).
Quemar las pestañas – To burn the midnight oil, to cram for a test.
Queque – Something easy, a piece of cake.
Quinada – Quinine water, soda.
Quitado – A boring person, someone who avoids participating.
Quitarse el tiro – To avoid a responsibility or to back out of a deal.

Rr

Rabo – Someone's rear end.
Radios or rayos – spokes
Ráfaga - Like a burst of bullets from a machineun.
Rajado – Incredible
Rajar - To brag.
Rajar de algo – To brag about something
Rajón – A braggart.
Rancho or Ranchito – 1. A structure with thatched-palm roof. 2 Vomit (vulgar).
Rata – A self-centered person, an egotist.
Rayar – To pass another car.
Recetar – To scold someone or sell drugs.
Recortar - To cut a budget.
Refor - Abbreviation for la reforma, Costa Rica's main prison.
Refresco – A cold drink
Refri - Abbreviation for refrigeradora (refrigerator).
Regalar – To have a baby.
Regañar - To scold.
Regar bolas – To spread gossip.
Regar las bilis – To get mad or irritated.
Regarse – To have an orgasm (vulgar).
Reguero – A big mess.
Rendija – Crack.
Repuestos – Repair parts (for cars, machines)
Reputear – To scare (vulgar).
Respaldar – To back or support someone.
Retorcer – To twist someone's arm or to wring their neck.
Reventada – A good looking woman.
Revolcarse en la tumba – To roll over in one's grave.
¡Rica! – Rica or delicious woman!
Ricura – Pleasant.
Ride – To give someone a lift.
Robacelus - A cell phone thief.
Robar cámara – To attempt to be the center of attention in every photo.
Robar oxígeno – To rob oxigen, to be old, or near death.

Robar pasto – Steal someone's lover.
Robarle el mandado – To rob or to steal something put into your hands or has been entrusted to you.
Robarle el mandado – To steal someone's girlfriend
Robo a mano armada – Armed robbery
Roco – An old person.
Rocola – Juke Box.
Rocolo – An old person.
Rodar – To deceive by stringing along.
Rogelio – A 1000 colón bill.
Rojo – A 1000 colón bill.
Rojos – 1. One red. 2. 1000 colones because it's a red bill.
Romper o partir la madre – To break someone's ass.
Romper su palabra – To break one's word.
Ron – rum
Ron con coca – rum and coke.
Ropa interior – a woman's underwear (panties and bra).
Ropero – Clothes closet.
Rosca – Male sex organ (vulgar)nts
Ruco – 1. Horse. 2. Pants.
Ruliar – To sleep.

Ss

Sacacorchos – Corkscrew.
Sacar caja – To puff out your chest pridefully.
Sacarle el jugo a algo – Take advantage of a situation.
Sacarle la tarjeta roja – To expel a player from a soccer game, to fire someone, or to end a relationship.
Sacarse el clavo – To avenge.
Sádico – A handsome man.
¡Salado! – Tough luck! Person with bad luck.
¡Soque! – Hurry it up!
¡Suave! – Take it easy!
Salir aventado – Quickly.
Salir con un domingo 7 – To do something stupid.
Salir de una y se mete en otra – To extract yourself from one problem and promptly become enmired in yet another drama.
Salirle el sapo a alguien – To put your foot in your mouth.
Salonear - To work as a waiter.
Salvada – Any action that gets you out of a jam.
Salvar – To get someone out of a jam.
Salvarle la tanda – To get someone out of a jam or to render aid.
Salvatandas – A savior or someone who extracts you from a jam.
Salveque – A backpack (mochilla).
Sampedranos – Residents of San Jose's suburb San Pedro.
Samueleador – A peeping Tom.
Samuelear – To spy on.
Sancochar – To steam vegetables.
Sangrón – Bully.
Santa Faz- An image (rosro) of the face of Jesus.
Santa Sede - The Holy See.
Santo con cachos – A devilish person.
Santo de cara - Good luck .
Santo de espaldas - Bad luck.
Santo de pajares- Someone whose sainthood can't be trusted.
Santo patrón- A patron saint
Santo y seña- A military password.

Santurrón - A hypocrite.
Sapear - To accuse or to tell on someone.
Sapitos – 1. Little toads. 2. Skipping stones across the water.
Sapo – 1. Toad. 2. A gossiper, a tattletale.
Sataneño or cebollero – Someone from Santa Ana (onion people).
Sátiro – A dirty old man.
Se cagó en la olla de leche. - To screw something up (vulgar).
Se despicho tere – Major fail.
Se divierte– To have a ball or good time.
Se falló – It failed.
Se fue de pollo or - To screw up, to have been deceived.
Se fue en todo - To screw up, to have been deceived.
Se hodió – it failed.
Se la juega – Know how to handle or manage something.
Se la pasa bien – To have a ball or good time.
Se la tira rico – To have a ball or good time.
Se le fue el santo al cielo - Someone forgot what they were saying.
Se le fue la mano – To get carried away or have your hand slip.
Se le fue la pájara – Some thing or someone got away from someone.
Se le fue la yunta - Your lover left you for good.
Se le mete el diablo - To get very angry or to temporarily go crazy.
Se merendo – Humongous. Massive.
Semana Santa - Holy Week .
Señor or Sr. – Mr.
Señora or Sra. – Mrs.
Señorita – A young unmarried woman.
Ser buena nota – To be a cool person.
Ser codo – A cheapskate.
Ser como ballena, que todo le cabe y nada le llena – Someone who eats a lot but is never satisfied.
Ser como carne y uña – To be good friends.
Ser el ombligo del mundo – To be the center of attention.
Ser pan comido – To be easily accomplished, a piece of cake.
Ser pipa – To be intelligent..
Ser todo oídos – To be all ears.
Ser todo un pegue – To be a success, or hit.
Ser torpe – To be all thumbs, clumsy.
Ser un santo- To be a saint, to be a good person.
Ser una pipa – To be very intelligent.

Serruchar el piso – To backstab.
Serrucho – Dog.
Servicio – A polite term for toilet.
Sicario – A paid assassin.
Sillín – A bike seat.
Sin cejas – Without eyebrows.
Sin pestañear – Without batting an eye.
Sin vela en el entierro - To lay the blame on an innocent party.
Sin vergüenza – A shameless person.
Sindi (sin dientes) - To be toothless.
Sobársela – To masturbate (vulgar).
Sobre – 1. Envelope 2. Bed.
Socado – Fast.
Socollón – An earthquake.
Soconear - To shake.
Soda – A small restaurant, diner or café.
Solo bueno! - Only good! or It's all good!
Soltar el perro – To pay a debt or someone you owe.
Soltar el pico – To talk or to spill the beans.
Sombra – 1. Shade 2. Jail.
Soplado – Fast.
Soplar – To tell on someone, to snitch.
Soplarse – To hurry.
Soque! - To hurry up!
Sordina – Deaf.
Sorry – Pardon me, sorry.
Sostienetetas – Brassiére as in a flaming. Brassier (vulgar).
Suave – A crybaby.
Suave – Soft. Suave mae! Take it easy man!
Subirse el apellido – To get mad.
Subírsele el humo a la cabeza – Success gone to the head.
Sudar la gota gorda – To work hard.
Sueta – sweater

Tt

Ta'bien – It's ok (abbrev Esta Bien).
Tabo – Jail.
Tachuela – Thumbtack.
Tacos – Soccer shoes.
Tafies – Fiesta or party, ie Fiesta pronounced backwards.
Tallado – Broke, no money.
Tallador – Brassiére. (Sostén).
Talonear – to walk fast or hurried.
Tama – Abbreviation for the beach town Tamarindo.
Tamagringo - The beach town of Tamarind.
Tamalear – To eat tamales.
Tamaño poco – A lot.
Tamarindear - To drink liquor.
Tanda – A drinking binge.
Tapa del perol – The best of the best. Lo mejor de lo mejor.
Tapia – Deaf.
Tapis – A drink of liquor or to be drunk.
Tapis – To be drunk.
Taquear – To eat tacos or get clogged (constipated).
Tarreado – Drunk.
Tarro – Jail.
Tata – Father.
Te conozco mosco – To know someone well.
Te tomo tu palabra – I'll take your word for it
Teja – 1. A roofing tile 2. A hundred colón bill.
Tele – Abbrev. for televisión or television.
Templado – Someone who gets sexually aroused easily.
Templarse – Get sexually excited (vulgar).
Tener buen culículum – 1. Wordplay on curriculum or resume. 2. A woman's shapely rear end.
Tener buena cuchara – To be a good cook.
Tener buena mano – To be good at something.
Tener chicha – To be angry.
Tener chispa – To be intelligent.
Tener cola – to have problems from the past.
Tener colmillo/colmilludo – Someone astute.

Tener filo – To be hungry.
Tener hasta el copete – To be fed up.
Tener la palabra – To have the floor (your turn to speak).
Tener la papa en la mano – Have something easy.
Tener las manos largas – To have sticky fingers (to steal).
Tener los días contados – To have your days numbered.
Tener más colmillo que un elefante – To be astute.
Tener más concha que una tortuga – To be shameless.
Tener más entradas que el aeropuerto Juan Santamaría – To have a receding hairline.
Tener más fe que San Roque – To be optimistic.
Tener todo el güevo – To a have a lot of money.
Tengala adentro – Keep inside, Procrastinate take your time.
Tenis – A woman's beasts (vulgar).
Terco/a– Someone stubborn.
Teresa – A woman's breast (vulgar).
Terraza cubierta – Porch.
Tetas – Tits.
Tetuda or tetona – Ample breasts.
Textear – To send a text message..
Tickete – Ticket
Tico – A Costa Rican.
Tierra Santa – The Holy Land.
Tieso – Broke or without money.
Tigra – Laziness.
Tija sillín – A seatpost.
Timba – A fat stomach.
Timbre – doorbell.
Tingo – a Tico/Gringo.
Tipo or tipa – a guy or gal.
Tiquicia - Costa Rica.
Tiquismo or costarriqueñismo – a Costa Rican expressio.
Tirar la toalla – To throw in the towel or to give up.
Tirarse a la pista - Without hesitation. 2. To dance.
Tirarse al agua – To make an attempt to accomplish a goal.
Tiro – Solution.
Todo el mundo – Everyone.
Todo el santo día - The whole day long.
Todo está a cachete – All is very good (la pura vida).

Todo terreno - 4WD vehicle-versatile, somone good at many tasks.
Tomarle el pelo a uno – To pull someone's leg or to tease.
Tombo – A policeman.
¡Tome chichi! – Take that!
¡Tumba la vara! – Stop bothering me!
Topador - Somone who sells stolen merchandise, a fence.
Toparse a bocajarro con alguien – To bump into someone.
Torcedura – A sprain.
Torcer – 1. To twist, twisting or turning.. 2. To wring out wet clothing or twist one's hands. 3. To steer to the right or to the left.
Torcerse – To sprain (an ankle or wrist).
Torcerse el pie – To go astray or to go wrong.
Torcidamente – Twisted.
Torcido – 1. Bad luck. 2. Crooked, corrupt. 2. A twisty road.
Torre – 1. A tower. 2. Someone's head.
Tortero – Someone who gets into lots of problems or caused them in the first place.
Tortillera – A female homosexual (vulgar).
Tortuguismo – A work slow down.
Tostado – Drugged or crazy.
Trabajar con las uñas – To work with very few resources.
Tragar grueso – To grin and bear it, to accept a fact you don't like.
Tragársela – To believe a lie or falsity.
Tragarse sus palabras – To eat your own words.
Traigo – An alcoholic drink.
Tramo – A type of stand used by street vendors.
Trasero – Rear end (on a car, human anatomy . . .).
Treinta y cinco – To be crazy.
Triciclo – A tricycle.
Trillo – A path.
Troleador – A walker.
Trolear – To walk or to go on foot.
Troles – Your feet.
Trompa – Mouth.
Trompudo – Big lips.
Trono – Throne or toilet.
Tuanis -A greeting: Great, Nice, Fantastic.
Tubo - Faucet.
Tubo inferior o diagonal – A bike frame's down tube.

Tubo superior – A bike's crossbar.
Tucán – A 5000 Colón bill.
Tucas – Tree trunk, describes a woman's nice looking legs.
Tuerca – A nut, as in nuts and bolts.
Tufo – A bad odor.
Tumba la vara! - Stop bothering me!
Turistear – To travel.
turisTICOS - Refers to tourism, a wordplay on tico tourists.
Turri – Abbreviation for the town of Turrialba
Turrialbazo – Describes Turrialba volcano spewing ash and rock.
Tuza – A good for nothing.
Twanys! – Everything's great!

Uu

U - short for universidad or university
Ultimar – To kill.
Un pájaro me dijo – By word of mouth.
Un pichazo - A large blow or a huge hit of something
Un puñado - A handful.
Un queque – Something easy to accomplish, a piece of cake.
Un toque – Wait a moment.
Una libra – Five-hundred colones (currency).
Una person 4 por 4 – Someone handy, a jack-of-all-trades
Uniciclo – Unicycle.
Untar la mano – To grease someone's palm, to bribe them.
Upe! – Hello, is there someone there? Anybody home? (Sarcastic)

Vv

Va jalando! - Get out of here! Go away!
Vaciar el saco - To get something off one's chest.
Vacilar – To deceive.
Vacilón – Fun.
Vaina – A thing.
Valpulear – To beat.
Válvula – Tire valve.
Vara – A thing or object.
Vararse – To have your car break down.
Varas – 1. Any situation or thing. 2. Just kidding.
Vaya busca brete! - Get a job!
Ventanear – To window shop.
Ve peluda – to be doing well
Ver los toros desde la barrera – To remain on the margins, to avoid danger.
Ver ventanas – To window shop.
Veranillo de San Juan – Indian Summer.
Verbalmente – By word of mouth or por otras bocas.
Verboso – Wordy.
Vergazo – A blow or hit. (vulgar).
Vergear – To beat someone (vulgar).
Vergear – To beat with a rod or hit someone.
Verla fea – To be in a jam.
Versele el pensamiento – To be so bald you can read their thoughts.
Vice – The vice-president of the country.
Victimizar – To victimize.
Vieja de patio – A gossip.
Viejo Verde – 1. Green old man. 2. Dirty old man.
Vieras – You should have seen. . . .
Vinear – To snoop.
Vino – A snoopy person.
Vino – Wine.
Vino blanco – White wine.
Vino tinto – Red while.
Vio 'ofe" – A play on words that means things turned out bad.
La vio cerca – To have seen death up close

Vivazo – An astute or sharp person.
Vivir cagado de risa – To laugh all the way to the bank.
Vivir horas extras – To be living on borrowed time.
Voladera de bala - A shootout, firefight.
Volar – To fire Someone.
Volar culo – To have sex (vulgar).
Volar pata – To walk.
Volar pedal – To ride a bicycle.
Volar pico – To talk
Volar piedras – To throw stones.
Volar plomo – To shoot.
Volar rabo – To fornicate.
Volar rueda – To drive a vehicle.
.Voló or la sacó del estadio - To screw something up.
Volverle la cara al revés – To turn someone's face inside out
Volvérsele la rosca – Transexual orientation (vulgar).
Vos – Familiar form used in place of tú.
Vuelta – An errand.
Vuelto – Change (money) from a transaction.
Vueltón – A long distance or trip.

Ww

Wacala – Gross!
Wachiman – A guard or watchman.
William – Wili
Wiski – Whiskey.

Yy

Ya me voy – I'm leaving now
Ya tiene cédula – To be an adult
Ya vengo – I will be right there.
Ya voy – I will be right there, on my way.
Ya! – Done, finished!
Yigüirro – A bird or homosexual (vulgar).
Yodo – Coffee.
Yugo – work.
Yunai - U.S.A. los Estados Unidos (EE UU).
Yunta – A romatic couple (people).
Yuyo – Someone who bothers you a lot or a pest.

Zz

Zafarse – To take off one's clothes.
Zaguate – 1. A mutt, street dog, 2. A womanizer.
Zaguate – Dog.
Zanja – A ditch
Zapatero a sus zapatos – Get to work!
Zaradajo – Old clothes, rags.
Zarpe – The last drink, one for the road.
¡Zócale! – Hurry up! Get the move on!
Zocar – To hurry.
Zocarse la faja – To economize
Zompopa – A big ant.
Zorra – A loose woman. Slut. (vulgar).
Zorrear – To look for women (vulgar)
Zorro – A girl-crazy man (vulgar).

Made in the USA
Coppell, TX
20 October 2020